Chasing the JERSEY DEVIL

Anna Anderhagen

Big Buddy Books
An Imprint of Abdo Publishing
abdobooks.com

abdobooks.com

Published by Abdo Publishing, a division of ABDO, PO Box 398166, Minneapolis, Minnesota 55439. Copyright © 2024 by Abdo Consulting Group, Inc. International copyrights reserved in all countries. No part of this book may be reproduced in any form without written permission from the publisher. Big Buddy Books™ is a trademark and logo of Abdo Publishing.

Printed in the United States of America, North Mankato, Minnesota
102023
012024

Design: Denise Hamernik, Mighty Media, Inc.
Production: Mighty Media, Inc.
Editor: Liz Salzmann
Cover Photograph: William/Adobe Stock
Interior Photographs: Daniel Eskridge/Alamy Photo, p. 25; Debby Wong/Shutterstock Images, p. 29; Heather A. Harvey/Adobe Stock, p. 27; Karrrtinki/Adobe Stock, p. 5; Library of Congress, pp. 9, 13; Made/Adobe Stock, p. 7; Michael Birts/Shutterstock Images, p. 19; Norm/Adobe Stock, p. 21; Philadelphia Bulletin/Wikimedia Commons, p. 15; PTZ Pictures/Adobe Stock, p. 11; Ryan Paul Marchese/Shutterstock Images, p. 17
Design Elements: Joko/Adobe Stock (tape and paper); Melica/Adobe Stock (polaroid frame); mizlatic/Adobe Stock (silhouette); Net Vector/Shutterstock Images (map); Oleg Iatsun/Shutterstock Images (compass); Piman Khrutmuang/Adobe Stock (paper); STILLFX/Shutterstock Images (background texture); TatianaMakhakhei/Shutterstock Images (footprints); Wandeaw/Shutterstock Images (background texture); Yevhenii/Adobe Stock (tape)

Library of Congress Control Number: 2023939279

Publisher's Cataloging-in-Publication Data
Names: Anderhagen, Anna, author.
Title: Chasing the jersey devil / by Anna Anderhagen
Description: Minneapolis, Minnesota : Abdo Publishing, 2024 | Series: Chasing cryptids | Includes online resources and index.
Identifiers: ISBN 9781098291907 (lib. bdg.) | ISBN 9781098278809 (ebook)
Subjects: LCSH: Jersey Devil (Monster)--Juvenile literature. | New Jersey--Pine Barrens--Juvenile literature. | Animals, Mythical--Juvenile literature. | Folklore--Juvenile literature. | Cryptozoology--Juvenile literature.
Classification: DDC 001.944--dc23

CONTENTS

CHAPTER 1

CHASING CRYPTIDS

You are walking in the woods when you hear a hiss. You look up and see a flying horse with horns! It jumps from tree to tree, looking at you with big red eyes. Suddenly, it flaps its huge wings, screams, and flies away! Could this be the Jersey Devil cryptid you have been looking for?

Over the years, the Jersey Devil has had many names, including "Leeds Devil," "Wozzle Bug," and "Hoodle-Doodle Bird."

CHAPTER 2

WHAT IS A CRYPTID?

A cryptid is an animal that has not been proven to exist. There are stories about many different cryptids. One of the oldest known cryptids is the Jersey Devil. But no one has been able to prove it exists.

Most people **describe** the Jersey Devil as having a horse face and bat wings. Some say it has horns and a tail. Others talk about its horrible screams.

CRYPTID PROFILE

NAMES: Jersey Devil, Leeds Devil, Hoodle-Doodle Bird, Wozzle Bug

CLASSIFICATION: mammal

COUNTRY: United States

HABITAT: forests

DESCRIPTION:
— horse's head
— large wings
— red eyes
— horns
— tail

PROVEN TO EXIST: not yet

THE JERSEY DEVIL'S ORIGINS

There are numerous stories of how the Jersey Devil was born. The most famous story takes place in Leeds Point, New Jersey. In 1735, a woman known as Mother Leeds gave birth to a child during a thunderstorm. That child became the Jersey Devil.

The Leeds house in Leeds Point, where the legend of the Jersey Devil may have started

CHAPTER 4

MYSTERIOUS FOREST

Most Jersey Devil sightings have been in or near the New Jersey Pinelands National **Reserve**. This large forest of tall pine trees is commonly called the Pine Barrens. The US Congress established it as a national reserve in 1978. The thick forest is a perfect **habitat** for a **spooky** cryptid like the Jersey Devil.

The Pine Barrens cover 1,100,000 acres
(450,000 ha) in southern New Jersey.

CANNONBALL TEST

In the early 1800s, US Navy officer Stephen Decatur visited Hanover Mill Works in Hanover Township, New Jersey. The mill made and tested cannonballs for the navy. While he was there, Decatur saw a flying creature that looked like a horse with wings. He fired a cannonball at it! The beast screamed and flew away. Decatur thought it was the Jersey Devil.

Decatur commanded ships in the US Navy. He was
considered a war hero.

CHAPTER 6

JANUARY 1909

There were more than 1,000 Jersey Devil sightings in January 1909. Many people saw it in southern New Jersey and Philadelphia, Pennsylvania.

One report was from the Evans family of Gloucester, New Jersey. A strange noise woke them up. They saw the Jersey Devil outside their window. It had large wings and made hoof prints in the snow!

A sketch of the Jersey Devil that appeared in the *Philadelphia Bulletin* in January 1909

CHAPTER 7

SIGHTINGS CONTINUE

Jersey Devil sightings have continued to be reported since 1909. In 1978, two teenage boys were ice skating near Chatsworth, New Jersey. They smelled dead fish and saw two red eyes staring at them. The boys were sure it was the Jersey Devil.

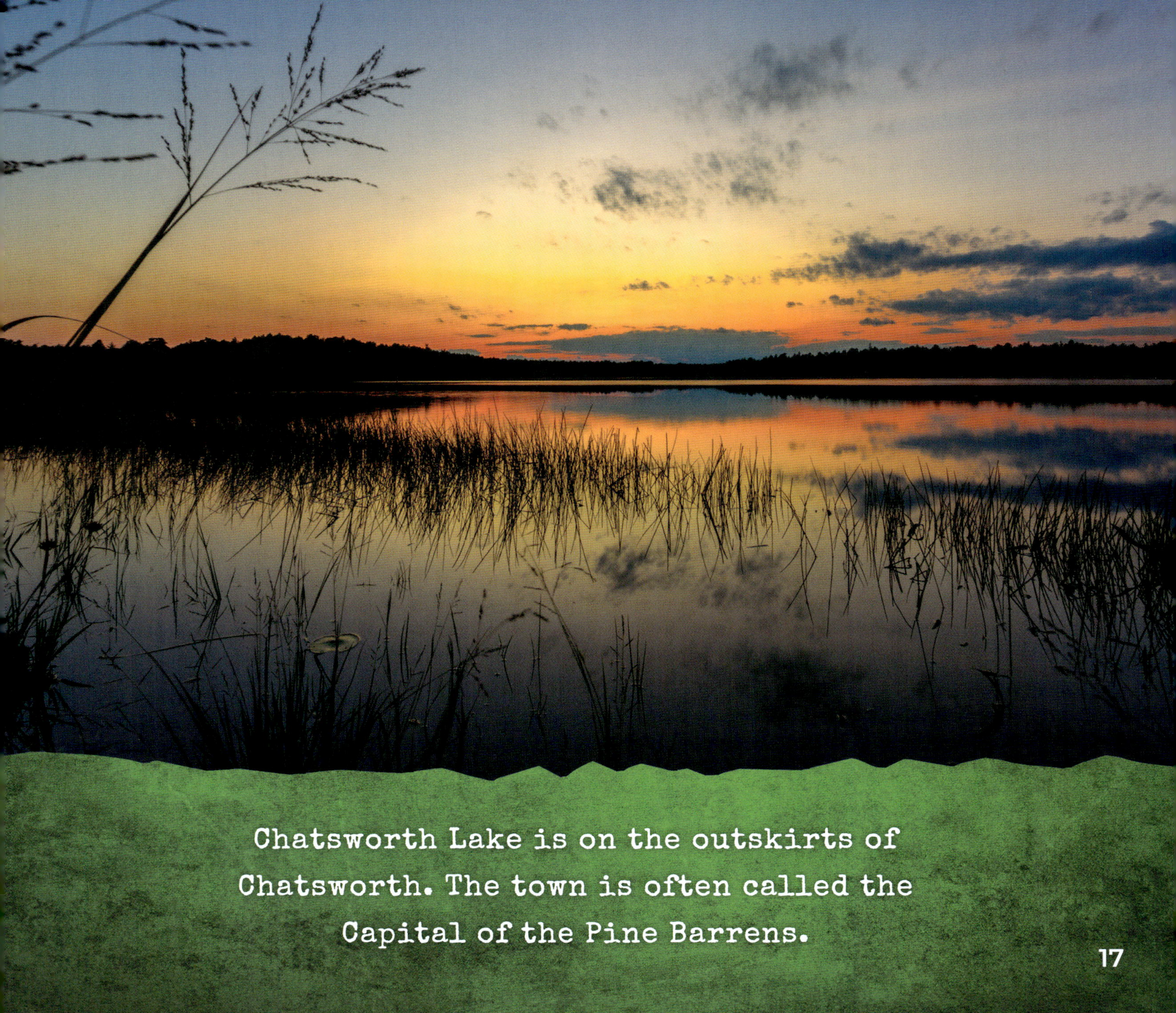

Chatsworth Lake is on the outskirts of Chatsworth. The town is often called the Capital of the Pine Barrens.

In 1993, forest ranger John Irwin saw the Jersey Devil in the Pine Barrens. He said it was six feet (1.8 m) tall with horns. He watched the creature run into the forest.

In October 2015, David Black was driving through Galloway Township, New Jersey. He thought he saw a llama walking in some trees. Suddenly, the creature spread its wings and flew away.

Irwin spotted the Jersey Devil near the Mullica River. The river flows through the Pine Barrens to the Atlantic Ocean.

CHAPTER 8

TRACKING THE JERSEY DEVIL

There is a group who call themselves the Devil Hunters. They want to discover the truth about the Jersey Devil. They go on hunts and outdoor **excursions** to find it. They do not want to capture or kill the Jersey Devil. They just want to answer questions about the creature and its **legends**.

The Devil Hunters search for the Jersey Devil
in places such as old, abandoned villages
in the Pine Barrens.

JERSEY DEVIL SIGHTINGS
PENNSYLVANIA
NEW JERSEY
Hazlet
Trenton
Burlington
Philadelphia
= one sighting
Leeds Point
Camden
Pine Barrens
UNITED STATES
N
W E
S
22

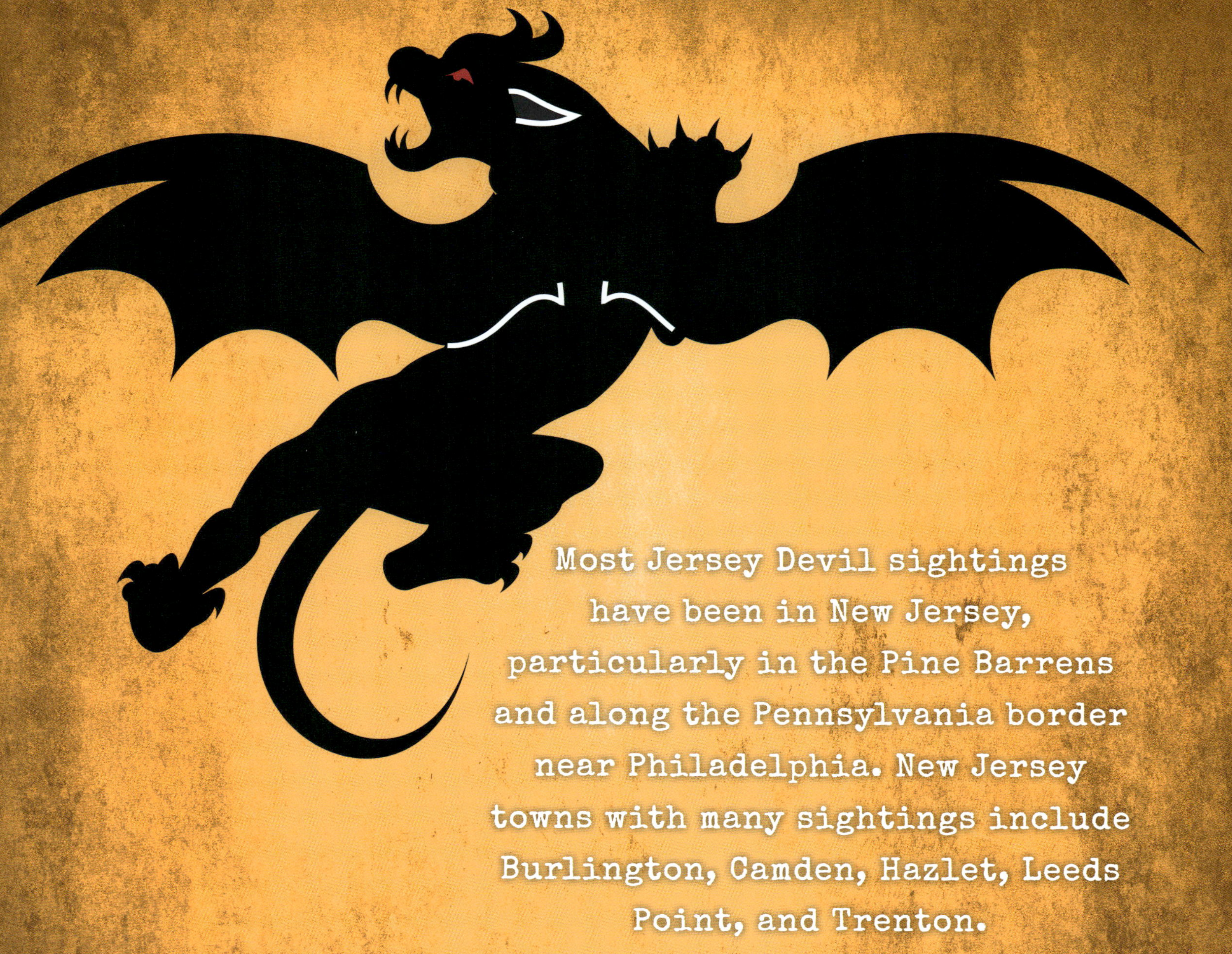

Most Jersey Devil sightings have been in New Jersey, particularly in the Pine Barrens and along the Pennsylvania border near Philadelphia. New Jersey towns with many sightings include Burlington, Camden, Hazlet, Leeds Point, and Trenton.

CHAPTER 9

CRYPTID KEEPER: LINDA GODFREY

Linda Godfrey spent 25 years chasing cryptids, including the Jersey Devil. She wrote 18 books on strange creatures. She was an **expert** in researching modern-day monsters, especially **werewolves**. She shared her stories about the Jersey Devil and other creatures across the country. Sadly, Godfrey died in 2022.

Godfrey got her start as a reporter for a newspaper in Wisconsin. In 1991, she was assigned to cover sightings of a wolflike cryptid called the Beast of Bray Road.

CHAPTER 10

STUDYING THE JERSEY DEVIL

Some scientists have suggested that the Jersey Devil could really be a bird, such as a sandhill crane. These cranes are sometimes seen in southern New Jersey. They are large birds with very wide **wingspans**. Sandhill cranes also make screaming sounds and hisses. Could the screams from the Jersey Devil really be from a sandhill crane?

Sandhill cranes can be 3 to 4 feet (0.9 to 1.2 m) tall
and have wingspans up to 6.5 feet (2 m)!

CHAPTER 11

DOES IT EXIST?

Many people think they have seen the Jersey Devil. There are **sketches**, posters, and blurry photos. But no one has been able to prove they are real.

Most scientists do not think the Jersey Devil exists. They believe its **physical** features would be impossible in a real animal. For example, if it were really part horse, it would be too heavy to fly. What do you think?

The legend of the Jersey Devil is so important to New Jersey that the state's professional hockey team is named the New Jersey Devils.

describe—to tell about something with words. Such a telling is a description.

excursion—a short trip or outing.

expert—a person with special skills or knowledge on a subject.

habitat—a place where a living thing is naturally found.

legend—an old story that many believe but cannot be proven true.

physical (FIH-zih-kuhl)—having to do with the body.

reserve—a special park where animals can live in safety.

sketch—a rough drawing.

spooky—strange or frightening.

werewolf—a person who can take the form of a wolf.

wingspan—the distance from one wing tip to the other when the wings are fully spread.

INDEX